Hurricane

This book is to be returned on or before
the last date stamped below.

305 433

Falkirk Council

Contents

A Deadly Storm

In October 1998 a **tropical storm** was brewing over the warm, southern Caribbean Sea. Within two days, it developed into one of the strongest and most deadly hurricanes ever recorded – Hurricane Mitch. Its winds were measured at 290 kilometres per hour. This is the story of Hurricane Mitch and the people who lived through its fury.

Map Key

- - - 🌀 ➤   Path of
           Hurricane Mitch

Gulf of Mexico

Florida

ATLANTIC OCEAN

Cuba

Ambergris Cay

Jamaica

Mexico

Belize

Caribbean Sea

Guatemala   Honduras

El Salvador   Nicaragua

N
W   E
S

PACIFIC OCEAN

The Hurricane Begins to Develop

On 8th October 1998 a weather system called a **tropical wave** started moving across western Africa. After leaving the coast, it crossed the Atlantic Ocean and moved into the Caribbean Sea. By 21st October 1998 thunderstorms and rainstorms had developed.

Weather forecasters at the National Hurricane Centre in Florida in the United States saw the first signs of Hurricane Mitch. It was about 580 kilometres south of Jamaica. By the end of the day, the storm was upgraded to a **tropical storm** and named Mitch.

What Are Hurricanes?

Hurricanes are large storms, also known as typhoons or tropical cyclones. They may be more than 480 kilometres across. They have spiralling winds of more than 320 kilometres per hour. The wind can force the ocean's water level to rise by 5 metres or more. Hurricanes also contain storm clouds that cause heavy rain and flooding.

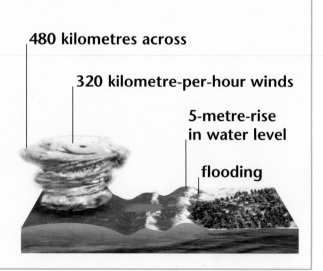

480 kilometres across

320 kilometre-per-hour winds

5-metre-rise in water level

flooding

NOAA forecasters monitor the direction of a hurricane.

Weather forecasters could not tell exactly how the storm would develop or the path it would take. They needed information to help them track the hurricane and give people time to prepare for its arrival.

Weather forecasters turned to the National Oceanic and Atmospheric Administration. NOAA sent specially trained pilots, known as storm trackers or hurricane hunters, to investigate the storm. The pilots flew planes filled with special weather instruments into the centre of the storm.

Where Do Tropical Storms Form?

Hurricanes form in tropical areas of the Atlantic Ocean over large areas of warm water. Strong storm systems that develop in the Indian Ocean are called tropical cyclones. Storms that develop over the Pacific Ocean are called typhoons. Scientists give each storm a name so that when two or more occur at the same time, they are easier to track.

Specially adapted planes fly in and out of a hurricane to collect information.

Monitoring Storms

Meteorologists use satellites and aeroplanes to monitor storms. A team of hurricane hunters flies in a specially adapted plane to the storm. Then they fly the plane in and out of the hurricane at least four times. This gives them information about the storm from four different directions.

Soon, the weather forecasters had the necessary information. They had information on the storm's size, wind speeds and air pressure. This information allowed scientists to measure the storm's force and predict where it might strike.

By 24th October 1998 scientists knew that Mitch had winds of more than 119 kilometres per hour. It was now officially a hurricane and it was heading towards Central America.

Preparing for the Hurricane

Emergency hurricane warnings were broadcast on television, radio and the internet. NOAA gave advice on how to prepare for a hurricane. People needed to get ready quickly.

George Parham was a hotel owner on Ambergris Cay (AM-buhr-grihs kee) in Belize. He had listened to all the weather reports. So when George heard that they had to leave Ambergris Cay, he was ready.

Belize includes many small islands called cays.

People were encouraged to leave Ambergris Cay for their safety.

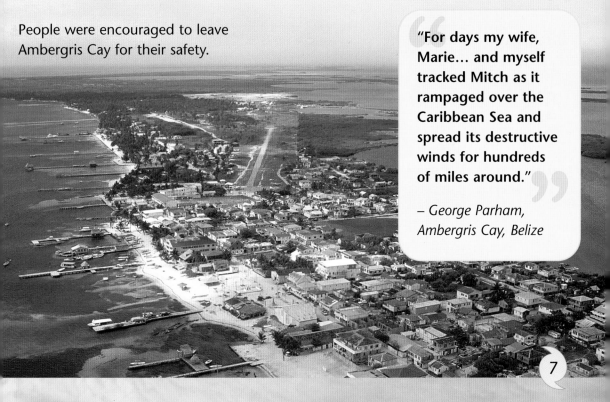

> "For days my wife, Marie… and myself tracked Mitch as it rampaged over the Caribbean Sea and spread its destructive winds for hundreds of miles around."
>
> – George Parham, Ambergris Cay, Belize

These people boarded up this building to protect it.

People living along the coast were told to leave their homes. Otherwise high tides and huge waves could drown them.

People living in river valleys were told to move onto higher ground. Otherwise they could drown in floods caused by the hurricane.

Windows and doors were boarded up with wood or metal shutters. This protected people and property against flying **debris**.

"Hurricane force winds extend up to 60 miles from the center... and tropical storm force winds extend up to 175 miles... Coastal flooding from strong onshore winds and dangerous battering waves is occurring over the coast of Honduras..."

– 26th October 1998, National Weather Service Advisory, USA

Evacuations Begin

In Honduras people were **evacuated** from their homes. Thousands of people were evacuated from coastal villages by the army and police. Hondurans living on islands off the coast were airlifted to the mainland.

In Belize, schools and other businesses closed. Buses took people inland to higher ground.

Hurricane Mitch headed towards Belize and Honduras.

Soldiers evacuated people from coastal villages in Honduras.

Stay or Leave?

Some people didn't want to leave their homes. Many of them boarded up their windows and stored food supplies and drinking water and stayed at home.

George Parham, the hotel owner on Ambergris Cay, Belize, was worried. He had decided it was too dangerous to stay on the island. However, several people arrived at the hotel asking for help, so George decided he would stay. He unlocked the hotel doors and took in the frightened people. Before long, the hotel was full. All they could do was wait.

> "We boarded up windows and so we were ready to leave. ...But evacuation was not to be for us."
>
> – *George Parham, Ambergris Cay, Belize*

People filled containers with water to prepare for the hurricane.

Waiting for the Storm

In Tegucigalpa (tay-goo-si-GAHL-pah), the capital city of Honduras, workers in a children's home called the Casa Alianza Crisis Centre prepared for Hurricane Mitch. They wondered if they would cope with the numbers of homeless children who might need shelter if the hurricane hit.

In Miramesi (meer-uh-MAY-see), people wondered if their homes would survive the storm. They were built along the river banks and were not very sturdy. If the river rose, then their homes might be flooded or destroyed. All they could do was wait and hope.

> "Rainfall totals of 15 to 25 inches… with locally higher amounts …are possible over the mountains of Honduras and other parts of Central America. These rains could cause life-threatening **flash floods** and mud slides."
>
> – 28th October 1998, National Weather Service Advisory, USA

Before Mitch struck, the Casa Alianza Crisis Centre could shelter 50 children.

Mitch Hits!

On 29th October 1998 the people in Central America prepared to face the fury of Mitch. All the experts had been right. The powerful Hurricane Mitch slammed into Honduras. Dangerously high winds and heavy rain lashed the coast.

Fierce winds and rain tore down trees and homes.

Heavy rain flooded and destroyed villages in Honduras.

Fortunately, Hurricane Mitch lost strength as it moved inland. Mitch moved over the central mountains of Honduras and Nicaragua. Heavy rain caused the most damage. It fell for three days and flooded the land.

Flooding caused dangerous conditions.

Few rainfall recording instruments survived. Those that did showed that in some areas almost 64 centimetres of rain fell over 36 hours. In central Honduras 50 centimetres of rain fell in only 12 hours. This was too much water for the land to soak up in such a short time.

Rising Waters

In Honduras Hurricane Mitch caused rivers to overflow. The water swept away buildings, roads and telephone lines. Schools and businesses closed as people fled from the mud and water. The bridge below was destroyed. People had to use a cage on a pulley to cross the river.

Mudslides

For years Hondurans have used trees for fuel and building materials. Removing the trees made the soil loose because there were no longer any roots to hold it in place. When the rain fell, the soil turned into a muddy liquid and slid downhill. Whole villages were then destroyed by these mud slides.

Heavy rainfall from Hurricane Mitch caused flooding in many areas of Belize.

Surviving the Storm

Although Hurricane Mitch did not hit Belize directly, the country still suffered damage from the rain, wind and **storm surge**. Trees were blown over and sand was shifted to new locations. On Ambergris Cay the people in George Parham's hotel looked out of the windows. Heavy rain poured down around them and huge waves pounded the island's shore.

Things returned to normal quite quickly on Ambergris Cay. It had been spared the full force of Hurricane Mitch. Soon people who had been **evacuated** returned home. Then everyone started cleaning up.

> "The rains fell in torrents continuously ...but we seemed to be snug in our fortress hotel."
>
> – *George Parham, Ambergris Cay, Belize*

Cars were abandoned as the flood waters rose higher.

Honduras was hit directly by the storm. Hurricane Mitch caused the river to rise by 18 metres. As the river flooded the roads, cars began to float. In the Casa Alianza Crisis Centre workers rushed to evacuate the children as the building started to flood.

"We were afraid because of the landslides," one fourteen-year-old said. "We saw houses falling down mountains..."

In Miramesi people found themselves waist deep in mud and rushing water. Huge boulders were washed down the raging river. Frightened villagers fled to the safety of higher land. They watched as their homes were swept away.

Swept Away

On 1st November 1998 Hurricane Mitch made its way out of Honduras into Guatemala and Mexico. It gathered strength again in the Gulf of Mexico, hitting Florida in the United States before losing strength.

Honduras suffered the most. Power and telephone lines came down. There was no electricity. Shelter, food and drinking water were in short supply. Disease began to spread.

Soldiers in the Honduran armed forces helped the storm victims. However, not everyone could be reached. Some villages were cut off by floods and collapsed bridges. Nevertheless, rescue workers did not give up.

Hondurans looked at some of the homes destroyed by a mud slide.

Before   **After**

Lush banana plantations were completely destroyed by the storm.

Most of the coffee plantations in Honduras were destroyed by Hurricane Mitch. Mud slides washed away the banana, pineapple and rice crops. Many coastal hotels were damaged. As a result, many people lost their jobs.

The economy of Honduras had depended on crops and tourism. Now the hurricane had destroyed many of the places where people worked. Still, the people were determined to rebuild their country. They also had the support of many countries from around the world.

Recovery

After Hurricane Mitch, Central America faced many problems. Thousands of people were left homeless. Many more were **displaced**.

In Honduras, and in other areas, the food shortage became worse. The Casa Alianza Crisis Centre was caring for twice the usual number of homeless children. But it was short of food and safe drinking water.

Workers at Casa Alianza kept going for long hours every day. Soon it had doubled its number of beds and found more workers to help.

Casa Alianza received aid supplies for many months after the hurricane.

Children at Casa Alianza slowly learned to smile again.

In Miramesi the houses were completely destroyed by the storm. They had been built with cardboard, plastic bags and mud. As the flooding stopped, people returned to their homes. Straight away they started rebuilding Miramesi.

People made temporary shelters.

Villages along the river banks were destroyed.

Boxes of food and medical supplies were flown in by plane.

World Aid

When rebuilding began, countries from around the world helped. They provided money, food, rescue equipment and help with reconstruction.

Food, medical staff, medicines, blankets and clothing were quickly flown in. Thousands of survival packs were dropped from the air into remote areas by rescue workers.

The Contents of a Survival Pack

+ Food for a family of six to last one to two weeks (beans, rice, sugar, flour, powdered milk, oil and coffee)

+ Water for drinking and washing

+ Basic medical supplies (bandages, ice packs, tape, creams)

+ Torches

+ Matches

+ Blankets

Despite the suffering caused by Hurricane Mitch, Casa Alianza survived and is still providing help to homeless children in Honduras.

Long-term plans for rebuilding Honduras were drawn up. In just a few years, people started building new homes, roads, bridges and sewage plants. They improved the farmland and planted seeds. Once again many families could feed themselves. Casa Alianza was rebuilt.

Miramesi also began to get back to normal. A teacher called Michael Miller started a housing project to help rebuild the area. It became a success story for Honduras and a model for the future.

Send a Teddy

Casa Alianza launched "Operation Bearlift" to cheer up the 100,000 children living in shelters. When people were asked to donate 100,000 teddy bears, they sent 300,000!

Glossary

debris   the broken, scattered remains of things

displaced   forced to leave one's home and unable to return

evacuated   moved away suddenly from an area, usually for safety reasons

flash floods   sudden, violent floods caused by heavy rain

meteorologists scientists who study the weather

storm surge   water that is pushed towards the shore by strong storm winds

tropical storm a system of strong thunderstorms with winds of 63 to 117 kilometres per hour

tropical wave a weather system in tropical areas with widespread cloudiness and showers

Index